The North of England
Early 19th Century

Newcastle

DURHAM
Stockton
Darlington

YORKSHIRE

West Riding

Preston
Blackburn
Bradford
LANCASHIRE
Bolton Bury
Manchester
Liverpool DERBYSHIRE

Cromford

LEICESTERSHIRE

Birmingham

N
W E
S

CHINA

Vladivostok

JAPAN

[TAIWAN]

Hong Kong

INDO-CHINA
PHILIPPINES

MALAYA

AUSTRALIA

NEW ZEALAND

Europe in 1750

NORWAY
SWEDEN
St Petersburg
Narva
Baltic Sea
Moscow

GREAT
BRITAIN
SCOTLAND

North Sea

DENMARK

RUSSIA

Glasgow

IRELAND

ENGLAND

EAST PRUSSIA

Birmingham
Cambridge
WALES
R.Thames
London

HOLLAND

Bremen
PRUSSIA
R.Oder
Berlin
Münden
Ruhr
SAXONY
Silesia
BELGIUM Düsseldorf
[GERMANY]
POLAND

N
W E
S

Abbeville

Rouen
Paris
Alsace-
Lorraine
R.Rhine

HABSBURG
EMPIRE

Combourg

Nantes
Le Creusot
AUSTRIA

FRANCE
SWITZERLAND

Montauban
Canal du Midi
Languedoc

ITALY

THE BALKANS

OTTOMAN
EMPIRE

TURKEY

〰〰〰 Boundary of the
Holy Roman Empire

I WAS THERE

INDUSTRIAL REVOLUTION

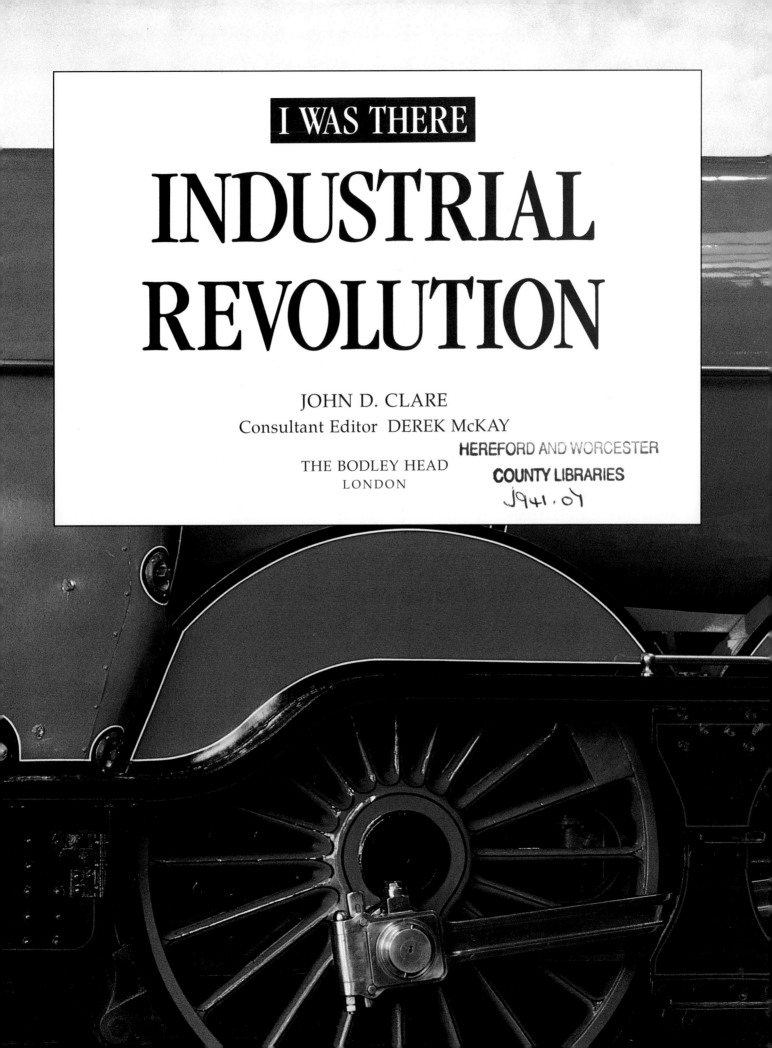

I WAS THERE

INDUSTRIAL REVOLUTION

JOHN D. CLARE

Consultant Editor DEREK McKAY

THE BODLEY HEAD
LONDON

First published in Great Britain in 1993
by The Bodley Head Children's Books
Random House UK Limited
20 Vauxhall Bridge Road, London SW1V 2SA

Random House Australia (Pty) Limited
20 Alfred Street, Sydney, NSW 2061, Australia

Random House New Zealand Limited
18 Poland Road, Glenfield, Auckland 10, New Zealand

Random House South Africa (Pty) Limited
PO Box 337, Bergvlei 2012, South Africa

ISBN 0-370-31835-8

A CIP catalogue record for this book is available from
the British Library.

Director of Photography Tymn Lintell
Photography Charles Best
Production Manager, Photography Fiona Nicholson
Designer Dalia Hartman
Visualizer Antony Parks
Editor Gilly Abrahams
Series Editor Helen Wire
Maps and Time-line John Laing
Map and Time-line illustrations David Wire
Jacket Concept Peter Bennett
Typeset 11/14 Palatino Sue Estermann
Reproduction Scantrans, Singapore

Printed and bound in China

ACKNOWLEDGEMENTS

Casting: Baba's Crew. Costumes: Val Metheringham. Make-up:
Emma Scott; Jane Jamieson. Picture Research: Lesley Coleman. Props:
Cluny South. Transport: Peter Knight, Road Runner Film Services.

Random House Children's Books would also like to thank:
Shelagh Ford, The American Museum in Bath; Tim Angel, Peter
Cameron, Libby Clonisey, Angels & Bermans; Philippa Gilbert, BBC;
Alan Cooke, BBC Radio; Sharon Brown and the staff at Beamish,
The Museum of the North; Douglas Hill, Beaulieu; Stuart Burrows,
Bath Industrial Museum, Mr Bowler's Business; Justine Burns; The
Cheadle Hulme Amateur Dramatic Society; Faith Eaton; Guy's and
St Thomas' Hospital; Robin Green, Catherine Pearson, Helmshore
Textile Museum; Andrea Hamblyn, The Imperial War Museum,
Duxford; Anita Fletcher, Jan Jennings, Mick Ward, Katie Foster and
the staff at Ironbridge Gorge Museum, Shropshire; Stephen
Atkinson and the staff at Liverpool Maritime Museum; Pru
Turnbull, Lovaine Trust Co. Ltd, Syon Park; Robert Aram, Masson
Mills; Paul Moore, The Museum in Docklands; National Railway
Museum, York; Mark and Sarah Hanna, The Old Flying Machine
Company, Duxford; Sarah Collins and the staff at Quarry Bank Mill,
Styal; Angela Murphy, The Science Museum; Angi Woodcock; and
the pupils of Greenfield Comprehensive School.

Additional photographs: Archiv für Kunst und Geschichte, Berlin,
p37 (left). Association of American Railways, Washington DC, pp28-9.
Beamish, p19. Susan Benn, pp38-9. Bridgeman Art Library, p18 (top,
National Railway Museum, York). The British Library, p63 (bottom).
Deutsche Fotothek, Dresden, p47. E.T. Archive, p40 (bottom). Mary
Evans Picture Library, p17 (top), p23, p26 (top), p40 (top). GEC-
Marconi, p37 (right). Hanwell Community Centre, pp46-7. Histor-
ische Archiv der Fried. Krupp AG, Essen, p7 (right). Hulton Deutsch
Collection, p26 (bottom). Illustrated London News Picture Library,
p53. Manchester Public Libraries, p63 (top). Mansell Collection, p63
(middle). Masson Mills, Derbyshire, front cover (background).
Museum of the City of New York, The Byron Collection, p43. National
Archives, Still Picture Branch, Washington DC, pp58-9. National
Museum of Wales, p30 (bottom). By permission of the Keeper of the
National Railway Museum, York, p57 (top). Rensselaer Polytechnic
Institute, Archives, Folsom Library, NY, p33 (exterior detail, photo-
graph by Irving Underhill). Royal Geographical Society, pp40-1.
Trustees of the Science Museum, p22, p54 (middle l. to r. 2, 3, 4;
bottom l. to r. 1, 3). Scientific American, Oct. 15 1853, plan by James
Swett, p29 (top). T.H. Shepherd, p7 (left). Trades Union Congress
Library, p48. Trustees of the V & A, painting by Samuel Scott, p10.

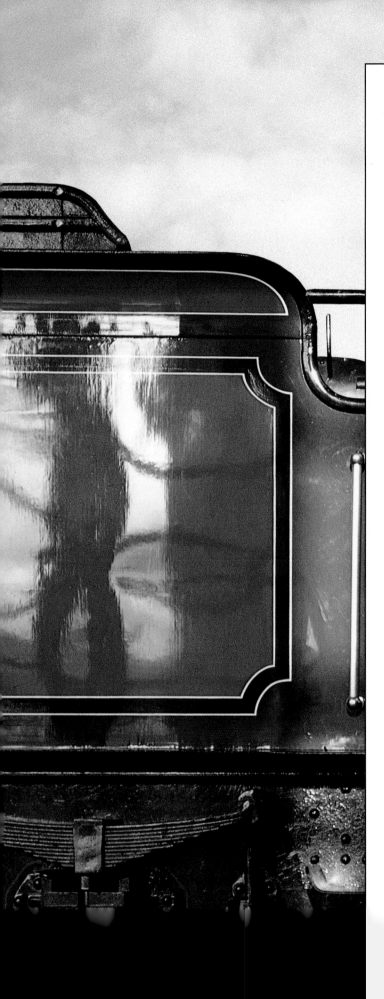

Contents

The Old Order

On 17 August 1896, Bridget Driscoll, a 44-year-old Irish woman living in London, became the first person in Britain to be killed by a motor car. The vehicle was travelling at 4 miles (6 kilometres) per hour. It had so amazed and terrified her that she had stood transfixed in its path and was knocked down.

Today, the world has changed. Motor cars are commonplace, mass-produced by robots. Food comes from a supermarket; you can pay by presenting the checkout assistant with a piece of plastic. On television, you can watch events as they happen all over the world – at any time of the day or night. In the privileged countries of the world, if your heart fails, it can be replaced by a healthy one.

The most amazing difference of all has been the quickening pace of change. The process of events which shaped the modern world began, in Britain, only two hundred years ago; one two-thousandth of the history of the human race. Today we expect and demand continuous improvement in technology and personal wealth.

Europe in 1750

Few things in 1750 would have amazed a man from the Middle Ages. Medieval woman would have thought very little had changed since her day.

The population of Europe was perhaps 145 million, less than the present-day population of Indonesia. Only 20 towns in Europe had more than 100,000 inhabitants. Nine-tenths of the people lived in rural areas and farmed to produce their food. They lived at subsistence level – producing just enough to feed themselves, and no more. During times of plenty, the population might grow. For a time the increase might be sustained as food was shared and living standards were lowered.

Eventually, however, war, famine or epidemic brought numbers back down.

Most of the states of western Europe were the private inheritances of individual ruling families. Germany (the Holy Roman Empire) was divided into some 350 principalities, duchies, counties and bishoprics (of which Prussia was the most important). Italy was similarly divided. In eastern Europe, the Ottoman and Habsburg emperors ruled huge empires. Like Louis XV of France, their rulers believed that they had a 'divine right' to rule their countries as they wished.

Ordinary people had little or no say in government. Britain had a parliament, but it was estimated in 1780 that only 214,000 men had the vote, out of a population of perhaps seven and a half million.

In most countries, wealth and power were concentrated in the hands of the nobility – at the most, perhaps 2 per cent of the population. In Hungary, the Estherhazy family owned 13,500 square miles (35,000 square kilometres) of land, an area the size of present-day Holland. In contrast, Poland had 3.5 million serfs; forced to live on their lord's estate, they were reckoned as part of its equipment. Serfdom was also common in Russia, Germany and the Habsburg Empire. Serfs could not marry or leave the village without their lord's permission. In Russia the law allowed nobles to do whatever they wanted to the ten million serfs; however, if the serfs made a complaint against their lord, they were sent to work in the mines or re-settled in Siberia! All serfs had to work, unpaid, for a number of days each week on their lord's estate – after 1775, a law in Germany and the Habsburg Empire tried to limit this to three days a week.

Industry was mostly restricted to western Europe and was small-scale. Large factories, such as the Van Robais textile mill at Abbeville in France, which had three thousand workers, were rare. The biggest glassworks in the Habsburg Empire had only 40 workers.

Trade was hindered by complicated systems of customs barriers. On the River Weser in Germany, there were 22 separate tolls between Münden and Bremen. As each stop took at least an hour, while the barge's entire cargo was inspected, a whole day was wasted simply paying tolls. Although some roads had been improved and a number of canals had been built – notably the Canal du Midi (1681) in the South of France – traffic still moved at the speed of the horse. It took two years to transport Russia's iron from the Ural Mountains, where it was produced, to St Petersburg, 1,000 miles (1,610 kilometres) away, where it was sold.

From the few, unreliable statistics that were recorded, it seems that in the mid-eighteenth century Holland was the richest country in the world, with an average income per capita (per person) of just over £8 a year. Britain came second (nearly £8) and France third (£6).

Most people lived in crushing poverty. In Poland, peasants lived on 'cabbage, sometimes potatoes, pease pudding, black bread and soup...'. In Montauban in France, the English traveller Arthur Young found 'a beautiful girl of six or seven years...smiling under such a bundle of rags as made my heart ache'. At Combourg, the people were 'almost as wild as their country, their town one of the most brutal, filthy places that can be seen; mud houses, no windows'. How could the local nobleman, wondered Young, 'have nerves strung for living amidst such filth and poverty?' There was nothing romantic or 'golden' about the period before the Industrial Revolution.

Industrial Change

In the late eighteenth century, Britain experienced a 'take-off' into economic growth. During the following century, industrialization spread, first to Belgium, France, Germany and the United States of America, and then gradually to many other countries.

Industry replaced agriculture as the main economic activity. Machines began to replace human skill and power. Iron and coal replaced wood. Trade increased, and transport and communications developed. The capital stock (machines and buildings) grew, and institutions were developed to finance the huge enterprises. Living and working conditions changed rapidly, and people's response changed governments and societies.

The industrial changes of the eighteenth and nineteenth centuries did not just expand the economy; they completely overturned the old order. For this reason they are called the Industrial Revolution (turning round).

The key development in canal building was the invention of the pound-lock in the sixteenth century. The lock is sealed at both ends by mitre gates (invented by Leonardo da Vinci). Water flows in or out, so that the barges can go up or down hills.

Above left: locks on the Regent's Canal, London, in the nineteenth century.

Above: 'Fritz', the huge steam-hammer installed at Krupp's steelworks in Germany in 1861 (see page 30).

The Domestic System

In the eighteenth century, most manufactured goods were produced by hand, in people's homes. In some areas, such as the West Riding of Yorkshire in the north of England, clothiers made their piece (of cloth) during the week, and sold it on Saturday at the local Piece Hall. In other areas, families who could not afford the raw materials were given them by an entrepreneur (businessman) called a putter-out, who collected and paid for the finished product at the end of the week. In Languedoc in the south of France a putter-out called Goudard employed six thousand spinners and weavers. The domestic system suited the employer, who did not have to lay out money to build a factory.

Beyond France and Britain, industry struggled or failed altogether. In Germany, it was restricted by powerful guilds, as it had been in the Middle Ages. In eastern European countries, such as Poland, there was almost no industry at all. To observers, it seemed that the fault lay in the character of the people. Polish industry was insignificant, reported the German traveller vom Stein in 1781, 'because the ordinary Pole is a careless being, who lives miserably and who knows no joy but wild living and drunkenness'.

The whole family takes part in cloth-making. Centre: the younger daughter brushes the cotton between two carding brushes to straighten the fibres into roving (thick bands of unspun fibres). Right: the mother and the elder daughter do the spinning (unmarried women are called spinsters). Left: the father weaves cloth on a hand-loom, while the grandmother winds thread and the son minds the baby in its cradle.

Although it is hard work – even the children often put in long hours – the family can start and stop working when they wish. In England, it is said that the men spend Sunday drinking, then take a holiday on Monday ('Saint Monday') to recover. When industry is thriving, the family spends more time making cloth; during a recession, they pay more attention to their small plot of land.

A tub in the corner is used to collect the family's urine, which they sell (at a penny a tub) to the local fulling mill, where it is used to bleach the woven cloth.

Trade and Growth

Historians do not know exactly when Britain's industrial 'take-off' happened. Nor do they know precisely when economic growth became self-sustaining (automatic and unstoppable).

Inventions were one of the results of the Industrial Revolution, not the cause. An invention is no use unless it is innovated (put into use).

What, then, led industrialists to innovate the new technology? The economic historian W.W. Rostow suggested that the key factor was a rise in investment (spending on new buildings and machinery) between 1780 and 1802. As businessmen invested their money, they employed more workers. When the workers spent their wages on manufactured goods, businessmen made a profit. They invested their profits, paying wages to more workers, who bought goods, and so on. In this way, a cycle of economic growth was created which became self-sustaining.

Yet what caused the growth in investment? Looking for an answer, historians have suggested many causes, going back further and further in history. Perhaps improvements in transport and agriculture in the eighteenth century reduced the cost of food, so people had money left over to buy manufactured goods. Perhaps the period of the Civil War (1642-60) broke down barriers in English society, so that nobles were not ashamed to invest in industry. Did the religious reformation of the sixteenth century create a 'business

ethic'? Some historians have traced the origins of the Industrial Revolution back to a burst of new ideas in the thirteenth century! Others suggest that the take-off was caused by a freak combination of all these factors.

In the eighteenth century, Britain's empire includes large areas of America and India. The Navigation Laws of 1651 and 1660 forbid the colonies to manufacture finished goods, and they have to buy their machinery, cloth and luxuries from Britain. The colonies have to send their produce – raw materials such as sugar, tobacco, coffee, flax and (in the warehouse, right) chests of tea and bales of cotton – to Britain.

Above: a painting of the Old East India Wharf, London. Between 1700 and 1772 the value of trade between Britain and her colonies quadruples to nearly £14 million a year. This trade stimulates the economy and creates in Britain a wealthy merchant class with money to spend and, perhaps, to invest in industry.

Inventions and Innovation

The first industry to mechanize in Britain was the cotton industry. The breakthrough was the innovation of the flying shuttle for weaving, after its invention in 1733.

Using the flying shuttle, weavers could work much faster, so they needed more spun thread; it took eight spinners to supply one weaver. A number of attempts were made, therefore, to invent a better spinning machine to increase the amount of thread available. In 1764 James Hargreaves invented the spinning jenny (see below). Five years later Richard Arkwright, a Preston wig-maker, invented the spinning frame (1769), which produced the thread by using rollers turning at different speeds. In 1779 Samuel Crompton of Bolton combined the moving carriage of Hargreaves' jenny with the rollers of Arkwright's frame to make the spinning 'mule' (so-called because a mule is a cross between a horse and a donkey). By 1812 there were thousands of mule machines, powering five million spindles. The new spinning machines were powered by water wheels and, in an increasing number of cases, steam engines.

For a while, there was a glut of thread. In 1820 there were a quarter of a million weaving looms in use, but they were not sufficient to deal with the vast amounts of machine-spun thread. Hand-loom weavers prospered. Confidently, they declared that 'never till they can make a loom talk and think can they invent one to weave by steam'. In 1785, however, Edmund Cartwright, a Leicestershire vicar, had invented a primitive power-loom and this was innovated in the years after 1830.

The new machines were hated and dreaded by the domestic workers. The hand-loom weavers, in particular, found themselves 'clothed in rags…sleeping on straw…working 16 hours a day', as they tried to make cloth as quickly and cheaply as the new looms. Their leaders urged 'war against the machines – yes, war to the knife'. Occasionally, mobs of machine-breakers (called Luddites after their mythical leader, Ned Ludd) rioted and wrecked the new machines.

The nineteenth-century historian Edward Baines, however, put the case for the new inventions. A single 100-horse-power steam engine could power fifty thousand spindles and produce 62,000 miles (100,000 kilometres) of thread in 12 hours – as much as 750 hand-spinners could produce in a year. This, Baines wrote in 1835, 'is the reason this industry can provide work and bread for more people… and of such results we should not complain'.

John Kay of Bury puts the shuttle on wheels – the flying shuttle – so the weaver (opposite page) can knock it to and fro, using a mechanism called a picker.

Below: legend says that James Hargreaves of Blackburn got the idea for his spinning jenny when he knocked over a spinning wheel; he puts the wheel on its side, so that it can turn 16 spindles at once. A moving clamp is pulled away from the spindles to stretch the roving into thread (left). Meanwhile, the spinner turns the wheel, which turns the spindles and twists the thread (centre). When the 'faller wire' is dropped onto the thread and the clamp moved back, however, the spun thread automatically winds onto the spindles (right).

The First Factories

The early inventions used what is called intermediate technology; they were ingenious devices but could be made fairly easily. This encouraged industrialists to introduce them. Arkwright employed a local clock-maker to make the first spinning frame. Cartwright remembered his first power-loom with embarrassment: 'The reed fell with the weight of at least half a hundredweight [25 kilograms] and the springs which threw the shuttle were strong enough to have powered a Congreve war rocket.'

The new machines were too bulky to be used in people's homes and too heavy to be worked by human effort. After 1781, when James Watt managed to turn the up-and-down movement of his steam engine into rotary (circular) movement, steam engines could be used to power the mules and looms. Such machines could only be housed in factories. In 1771 Arkwright built a cotton factory in the village of Cromford in Derbyshire. Other industrialists followed his example. Because of Arkwright, wrote a contemporary, 'the simple peasant is changed into the impudent mechanic'.

Minding the machines was desperately

dull work, and at first people resisted employment in the factories. To attract workers, Arkwright had to build houses for his employees, a church and an inn. When mobs threatened the mill, he collected 1,500 pistols, 500 spears and a number of cannons to defend it!

For the first time textile workers travel from their homes to 'go to work' – a completely new idea for most people. The structure of the workforce also changes. Older men find it hard to get a job in the mills. Joining broken threads and sweeping under machinery can be done by women and children, who are cheaper to employ than men, and easier to discipline.

A normal working day is 14 to 16 hours long. These workers are eating their breakfast during their quarter of an hour break at 9 a.m. They have already done three hours' work. The steam engine determines the work periods; all the machines stop and start at the same time. The concept of time enters people's lives. They 'clock on' and 'clock off' at the factory, and are paid according to the number of hours worked (instead of by the piece). As the overseer is often the only person with a watch, he decides when work starts and finishes, and who is late and will be fined.

Gradually, factory owners come to control their workforces completely. Arkwright's partner, Jedediah Strutt of Derbyshire, fines his young workers for even minor misbehaviour such as 'calling through the window to soldiers…riding on each other's backs… terrifying S. Pearson with an ugly face…and putting Josh Haynes' dog into a bucket of hot water'.

Coal

A 40-horse-power Watt steam engine (see page 14) working for 15 hours used 2 tons of coal a day. Factories, therefore, needed to be near a coalfield.

Meanwhile, changes in the iron industry also increased demand for coke (coal from which certain gases have been removed by heating). Since the Middle Ages, iron had been produced by smelting (melting) the ore using charcoal (which is made from wood). A shortage of wood, however, had led in 1784 to Henry Cort's discovery of how to make wrought iron using coke. Air heated by the coke was passed over the iron while a workman puddled (stirred) the molten metal with a long pole.

As a result of these developments, the coal industry expanded. Coal output increased from 11 million tons in 1800 to nearly 34 million tons in 1840.

Unlike other industries, the British coal industry did not introduce any major innovations. The coal continued to be hewn (dug out with pickaxes) by filthy, wet, naked miners working in seams that were sometimes only 0.6 metres (2 feet) high. Greater output was achieved simply by digging deeper. This increased the danger for the workers. On the Newcastle coalfield in the north of England, 1,468 miners died between 1799 and 1840. They were killed by explosions, suffocating

chokedamp (carbon monoxide), collapsing roofs, flooding, and runaway trucks.

In Britain, until the Mines Act of 1842, women and young girls, sometimes only 12 years old, drag the coal to the mine shaft. Even younger children also work underground, minding the trap-doors which direct a flow of air through the tunnels. They sit in the pitch dark, listening to the rats scurrying and the layers of rock settling. 'It does not tire me, but I have to trap without a light and I'm scared – sometimes I sing,' confesses Sarah Gooder, aged eight.

Right: most deaths in British mines occur from explosions caused by firedamp (methane gas). This builds up in areas of the mine that have not been properly ventilated, perhaps because a 'trapper' has forgotten to close a trap-door. The invention of the Davy safety lamp (1815) actually increases the number of deaths, because it allows 'fiery' pits to be worked

more extensively. Firedamp causes only a small explosion but it whips into the air large amounts of coal dust, which – as each speck is surrounded by a pocket of air – is also explosive. This leads to a second, more destructive explosion.

The First Railways

As early as 1700, on the Newcastle coalfield, there were many wagonways, along which ponies pulled coal from the mines to the ships which carried it to London.

Steam engines had been used to drain the collieries since 1712, and after the 1780s they were used to wind men up and down the shafts in 'cages'. Each colliery employed an 'engine-tenter' to look after the engines. These men began to experiment with moving steam engines, using the power of the engine to drive the wheels. In 1821 George Stephenson, enginewright at Killingworth Colliery near Newcastle, was invited by local businessmen to build a railway between the South Durham coalfield and the port at Stockton.

At first, the railways were opposed by canal owners, who feared for their livelihoods. Farmers claimed that the railways would destroy agriculture; cows would stop producing milk, hens would stop laying and the grass would wither and die, they said. Country people thought the fiery trains were the devil. Stephenson steadfastly ignored all the criticism. On one occasion he was quizzed by a Member of Parliament who wanted to prove that the railways were unsafe: 'Suppose now…that a cow were to get in the way of the engine – would that not be an awkward circumstance?' 'Very awkward',

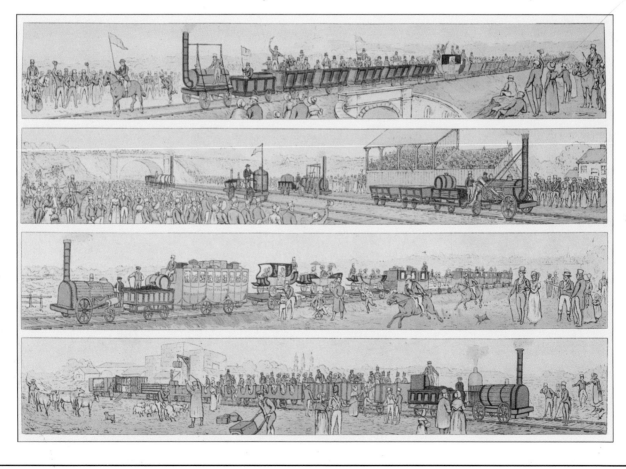

Stephenson replied, 'for the cow.'

In 1826 Stephenson began to build the Liverpool to Manchester Railway, the world's first passenger line operated solely by steam locomotives. He and his son built a number of other lines, including the London to Birmingham Railway (1838); 112 miles (180 kilometres) long, it took 20,000 navvies four years to build it and cost £5.5 million (see page 34). It was said to be a greater undertaking than the Great Wall of China.

When Stephenson retired in 1840, he had assured the future of the railways. In 1870, in Britain, 423 million passengers travelled on 16,000 miles (25,500 kilometres) of line.

The railway is the coming together of all the developments in steam, coal, iron and investment. Below left, top: Stephenson's *Locomotion* (also shown right) pulls the train on the opening day of the Stockton and Darlington Railway (1825), the world's first steam-hauled public railway. The lower pictures show the Rainhill locomotive trials (1829), and the first- and second-class carriages on the Liverpool to Manchester Railway (1833). Above left: the Primrose Hill tunnel (1837).

Engineering

As industry and transport adopted the new technology, it created a need for a new skill – engineering.

Firms such as the Whessoe Iron Foundry in Darlington, which supplied the Stockton and Darlington Railway, had to overcome the difficulties of making adequate rails, wagons, wheels, boilers, tubes, steam gauges and turn-tables. The parts had to bear the stresses of accelerating, braking and crossing bridges at speeds up to 60 miles (97 kilometres) per hour.

A similar process was happening in the cotton industry. As factories were built, firms were set up to make, install and mend the machines. By 1839 one engineer, Charles Fairburn of Manchester – who had started in 1816 with a shed, a lathe and 'a strong Irish man to help with the heavy work' – employed six hundred men in a large factory.

Engineers realized that inaccuracy caused fatal accidents and that the cause was not poor workmanship but poor tools. If the first stage of the Industrial Revolution was inventing machines to do the work of men, the next step was inventing machine-tools to make the machines. Engineers developed machines for boring (1774), making screws (1800), planing wood (1802), cutting gears (1820), grinding (1834), and shaping (1836). In the United States, the inventor Eli Whitney developed the idea of machines with inter-changeable parts; the 'American System' was soon introduced into Europe.

A group of journalists is being shown round an engin-eering workshop by the foreman (centre). The latest gear-cutting machinery, in this well-run establishment, under the management of an efficient businessman, will be the subject of newspaper articles which will interest many readers.

The group includes a foreign visitor, who seems particularly observant.

The Revolution Spreads

By 1800, British manufactured goods were flooding into European markets. To compete with low-priced British goods, European businessmen tried to industrialize.

A stream of entrepreneurs visited Britain, including the first French locomotive builder Marc Séguin (who spent some time working for George Stephenson), and the German engineer Alfred Krupp, who toured Britain under the name of Schropp. Alarmed at Britain's growing power, the Prussian government sent dozens of industrialists, civil servants and industrial spies (some of whom lived permanently in London).

European workers, however, found it hard to adapt to industrialization, and the attempts to acquire British know-how often failed. The first Prussian-built steam engine (a copy of a British machine) was made at an ironworks in Prussian Silesia. It took three years to build it (1788-91), and another year to transport it down the River Oder, across the Baltic and North Seas, and up the Rhine to the Ruhr. By the time it arrived, it was no longer needed!

One answer was to employ British workers and expertise. In 1785, the French government employed the English ironmaster William Wilkinson to set up their ironworks at Le Creusot; in the early years of the nineteenth century half its workforce of six hundred men were British.

In Belgium, the Cockerill family from Lancashire built a woollen mill, then moved into iron-making, engineering and armaments. They built the first locomotive on mainland Europe (1835) and had a hand in founding the *Banque de Belgique*. Cockerill used British technology, boasting that he had 'all the new inventions over [in Belgium] ten days after they come out in England'.

Industries that had been 'planted' frequently collapsed when the British workmen returned home. European employers also complained that the best men stayed in Britain – 'it is the rejects who come to us'. One German engineer longed for the day when 'the Englishmen can all be whipped out – we have to tread softly with them; they quit if you even look at them in an unfriendly way'.

New Industrial Countries

After Britain, Belgium was the first European country to industrialize. Coal production grew; steam engines were introduced into Belgian mines in 1720. The textile industry

prospered between 1806 and 1814, when Napoleon forbad imports of English cloth as part of his strategy to defeat Britain during the Napoleonic Wars. The Belgian engineering industry exported machines to the rest of Europe, and Belgian mechanics (like the English workmen) were employed in Germany and Austria; the Belgian engineer Jean Wasseige built the first steam engine in Germany, in 1751, for a lead mine near Düsseldorf.

Germany also began to industrialize in the early nineteenth century. Cotton-spinning was already done in factories; the first mill, with a water-powered Arkwright frame, was built in 1794 at Kromford (appropriately, see page 14), near Düsseldorf. After 1818 the German states began to form a *Zollverein* (a union for free trade); by 1834 most of the German states belonged to it. In 1826, when 14-year-old Alfred Krupp inherited his father's iron foundry in the Ruhr, he had only seven workmen. By 1835, business was growing, and he changed the factory from water-power to steam.

In France, businessmen were more cautious but growth was steady. A textile industry grew up on the coalfields of the north-east and iron was made in Alsace-Lorraine. In 1841 an English visitor declared that the French engineers were as good as the Belgians, and that their machines looked better – 'but that is merely French polish, not in the real fitting up of the machine'.

The United States

Until the end of the American War of Independence (1783), America was a British colony. It supplied Britain with raw materials – cotton, tobacco, rice, leather and meat – in return for manufactured goods. Even after the war, British industrialists consciously tried to destroy American industry, to keep the United States as a supplier country.

The population of the United States, however, was growing rapidly – from four million in 1790 to seven million in 1810 – and gradually American manufacturing developed to supply this huge market. British expertise was important in this initial industrialization. The first American cotton mill was built in Rhode Island in 1790 by Samuel Slater (an apprentice of Jedediah Strutt) who had memorized the details of how to construct Arkwright's spinning frame. The first American canals were built by British engineers, and Canvass White, the American surveyor of the important Erie Canal, had spent a year in Britain studying British canals.

The United States, however, was a country which had just won its independence from Great Britain. Industrialization was welcomed because it was seen as part of an exciting new way of life in a new world. Between 1820 and 1840, investment in American industry rose from $50 million to $250 million. The United States and western Europe began to modernize, gradually catching up with, and then overtaking, Britain. Innovative American businessmen contributed ideas and inventions to the development of the Industrial Revolution from its beginning.

Above left: the *Forge Anglaise* (English forge) at Le Creusot, in 1827.

Far left: machine tools made at Joseph Whitworth's engineering factory in Manchester, on show at the Great Exhibition at the Crystal Palace, London, in 1851. Exhibitions such as this publicized British technology.

Factory Work

Supporters of the factory system claimed, with some justification, that workers who had no employment did not frolic on the hillside but starved by the roadside, and that

schoolmasters were far more likely to use the strap than factory overseers. The English writer Andrew Ure assured his readers that, even for children, tying threads was not hard work: 'It was delightful…to see them at leisure after a few seconds' exercise of their tiny fingers.'

Most nineteenth-century factories, however, were grim, brutal places. In 1835 the French writer L.R. Villermé watched workers in Nantes walking to the factory – a journey which added an hour each way to their daily shift of 14 or 15 hours. 'It is worth recalling that legislation fixes the working day even for convicts at 12 hours,' he observed.

Cotton factories had to be kept hot and wet to stop the threads from snapping, so textile workers who had to walk home through the cold night air tended to catch pneumonia. They also suffered from a respiratory disease called byssinosis caused by the cotton dust. None of the machines had safety guards, so accidents were common amongst the ragged, long-haired workers, especially the young 'scavengers' who swept the waste from under the machines.

Children, who had to stand all day (which Villermé regarded as 'torture'), suffered from knock-knees or bow-legs. Punishments included being beaten with a strap or thrown into tubs of water. In one British workshop a boy who worked too slowly had his ear nailed to the bench. Beatings and accidents increased towards the end of the long working day. Girls became mothers knowing nothing but the inside of a factory. Boys,

sacked at the age of 17 or 18, often lapsed into crime, violence and alcoholism.

Although conditions improve as the century progresses, larger, faster machines are introduced which make the work even more demanding, while wages (being handed out by a clerk, above left) remain low. One female cotton worker complains that, although the working day had been reduced to ten hours, she works 'as if the Devel was after us…what with the heat and the hard work and all this is Done in Christian England and then we are tould to Be content in the station of Life to wich the Lord as places us But I say the Lord never Did place us there so we have no Right to be content'.

Left: the mill office from which the manager maintains strict discipline. In one cotton mill office in Lancashire, England, the clerks work in silence from 7 a.m. until 6 p.m. They each have to bring 4 pounds (2 kilograms) of coal a day for the stove. 'Calls of nature are permitted and the staff may use the garden.'

Urban Conditions

The population of the industrial towns grew rapidly, partly because of the steady migration of people from the countryside. The centres of these towns reflected the wealth industrialization had created; they had well-paved roads, magnificent town halls, luxurious stores, and fine statues financed by public subscription.

This, however, was the age of 'two nations'. Away from the main streets were blackened factories, slag heaps, open sewers and the hundreds of cramped courts (alleys) where most people lived in overcrowded, badly built houses. In 1835 a Frenchman, Dr Guépin, described the Rue des Fumiers in Nantes: 'Pass through one of the drain-like openings, below street level, that lead to these filthy dwellings…Feel one's foot slip on the polluted ground. Foul water oozes

out of the walls…Go in, if the fetid smell which attacks you does not drive you back… You will see two or three rickety beds with worm-eaten legs, a mattress, a tattered blanket of rags…'

Workers crowded together to save money on rent. As late as 1893, a German textile-worker described a house in Berlin: in the

attic the landlady slept with her 14-year-old son on a straw mattress; her niece shared the back room with a 60-year-old man and a 15-year-old laundress; in the front room, the landlady's brother slept on the sofa and her nephew (who paid extra to keep his suitcase in the room) had a hammock. On Sundays the front room was let out to a professional fortune-teller. In such an environment alcoholism was common; writers of the time described how husbands escaped to the tavern, leaving their embittered wives to look after the children.

Nineteenth-century town councils did not create these slums on purpose; they were just overwhelmed by the growing population. Bradford in England was the centre of the world's woollen industry. Its population in 1780 had been about 8,700. By 1841, with a population of 66,718, it had outgrown the sewage system to such an extent that in certain places the canal water was almost solid with human excrement and industrial waste. So many 'offensive gases' were produced that in hot weather the water sometimes caught fire. In a slum area downstream, the Irish immigrants took their drinking water from the canal.

Polluted drinking water caused epidemics of dysentery, typhoid and, notably, cholera, which swept Europe in 1830-32, 1848 and 1862-63. In the cold, damp rooms medical complaints such as rheumatism, bronchitis and tuberculosis were endemic (always present). Neither the employers nor the state paid workers when they were sick, so illness forced families to give up even cheap lodgings.

In 1851 there are few sewers in London. Human excrement from the privies (latrines) collects in cesspits, where it is cleaned out by nightmen (above left). This produces such an appalling smell that they are forbidden to work by day.

Filth, disease, crime and overcrowding are still problems in 1889 (left). Only slowly do councils introduce improvements such as gas lighting (right; see page 37), sewers and water mains (see page 53).

The Railways

British engineers built railways all over the world. Between 1834 and 1868, Thomas Brassey, an Englishman who had worked with George Stephenson, built 34 railways, comprising 2,800 miles (4,500 kilometres) of track, in Europe, Canada, Russia, Argentina, India and Australia. To build the Paris-Rouen line in 1842, Brassey employed 4,000 British navvies; they were the despair of the local police. British engineers also provided engines for Europe's railways; in 1845, out of the 487 locomotives in Germany, 237 were British.

British engineers also influenced the first American railway builders; John Jervis, chief engineer of the Delaware and Hudson Company, for instance, bought his first locomotive, the *Stourbridge Lion*, from England. Soon, however, American engineers began to build their own engines; the first were *Tom Thumb* and the *Best Friend of Charleston* (1830).

Railway 'mania' swept the world. The first American transcontinental line was laid by two companies; they started building from both coasts and officially met at Promontory Point, Utah, on 10 May, 1869. The two work gangs had actually met a month before, but (because they were paid by the mile) had simply continued building; 225 miles (362 kilometres) of parallel track had been laid before they were stopped. By 1900 there were 200,000 miles (320,000 kilometres) of track in the United States. In 1910 the European network comprised 170,000 miles (275,000 kilometres) of track. Six years earlier, even backward Russia had completed the Trans-Siberian Railway from Moscow to Vladivostok. It was the second attempt; initially the track had been laid in winter across the ice of Lake Baikal, and in spring a train had crashed through the ice and been lost.

The railways stimulated those industries which supplied materials and expertise – brick-making, the coal and iron industries

(see page 30), mechanical engineering and civil engineering (see page 32). The large amounts of money needed to finance the railways contributed to the growth of stock exchanges (see page 34).

Freight costs fell, reducing prices. Transport became faster; fresh food, notably milk and meat, could be brought into the cities, improving people's health. Communications improved; the postal services used the railways, and the telegraph was first developed to improve communication between stations in order to increase safety on the railways. Fear of trains running into each other also led to the introduction of a standard 'railway time' across Europe and the United States.

Irish, Italian, Polish and Chinese navvies build the American railways. Although attacked by buffalo and scalped by Indians, they lay up to 10 miles (16 kilometres) of track a day.

The railways unify the United States, bringing law and government to the territories of the Wild West. They make the Great Plains available for farming and link the industry of the eastern United States with the gold mines of California, the cattle ranches of Texas and the coal mines of Philadelphia. In this way, railways provide both raw materials and markets for industry. This, along with the rapidly growing population, enables the economy of the United States to grow faster than that of any other country.

Above: a design (1853) for an elevated railway.

Iron and Steel

The railways stimulated industry in Germany more than anywhere else. In 1851, 90 per cent of German iron was still made using charcoal, and German delegates at the Great Exhibition in London believed that 'Germany will never reach the level of coal and iron currently produced in England. We do not have the resources.'

In the twenty years after 1850, however, nearly 9,000 miles (14,500 kilometres) of railway were built in Germany. Seventy-five new companies were set up to make the iron for the rails, trains and rolling stock. Most were joint stock companies (see page 34) and some were huge – the Hörder Verein works in the Ruhr employed 1,700 workers. Business boomed. In one year alone Alfred Krupp (see page 23) added 300 iron-ore mines, two foundries and a fleet of ships to his industrial empire. All the new foundries used coke to smelt the iron, so by 1870 coal output had increased 600 per cent, and Germany was producing almost twice as much coal as France.

German engineering developed. At the Paris Exhibition of 1867, visitors marvelled at Hörder Verein steel plates, and at German military armaments such as a 50-ton Krupp cannon which fired 1,000-pound (450-kilogram) shells. Four years later Prussian troops destroyed the French army and, in the Hall of Mirrors at Versailles, a united German Empire was triumphantly proclaimed.

Britain was still economically stronger than Germany at this time. The German economy, however, was growing at 10 per cent per annum, a rate matched only by the United States. 'Today, you must be a businessman and make money, and wear a new coat and your hair short like everyone else, or you will be laughed at,' complained one young German. Bismarck, the German chancellor, preached 'blood and iron' (referring to war), but Germany's success, commented the economist J.M. Keynes, 'was built more truly on coal and iron' (industrial power).

Iron, smelted in a furnace, is poured into a mould (right). The lower half of the mould has been formed in the wet sand beneath. Cast iron is so cheaply and easily produced that it is used for a whole range of items, from fire engines to fireplaces (above).

Left: the open-hearth furnace at the Llanelly steel works in Wales, photographed in 1907. Steel is a form of iron which has been hardened by being heated with carbon and suddenly cooled. It is much stronger than cast iron and more malleable (able to be moulded) than wrought iron.

In 1856 Henry Bessemer, a German living in England, discovers a cheap way of making steel, using the Bessemer Converter. Most German firms, however, do not adopt the Converter. This works to their advantage, because after 1867 they are able to introduce the improved Siemens-Martin open-hearth process.

Civil Engineering

Railway-building stimulated the development of civil engineering, as railway engineers found ways to cross marshes, tunnel through hills and cross rivers. In 1825, the engineers of the world's first railway bridge, built for the Stockton and Darlington Railway over the River Gaunless, used four spans for a bridge only 15.2 metres (50 feet) wide. Fifty years later, at St Louis in the United States, James Eads built a steel-arch bridge which crossed the Mississippi in three spans of 152 metres (500 feet). It was estimated to be able to support a maximum weight of 173,832 tons.

Before long, steel was being used for other structures. In 1889, in Paris, Gustave Eiffel built a tower of steel. It is 300 metres (984 feet) high, weighs 18,000 tons, and has 12,000 struts and 2,500,000 rivets.

American architects began using steel frames for all large buildings, attaching the walls to the frames. Because the hydraulic lift had been developed (1857), they were able to build 'skyscrapers'. This method of building was called Chicago construction, because the first skyscraper was the Home Insurance building in Chicago (1885). The same principle, but using wood and nails instead of steel girders and rivets, was applied to ordinary housing and was called 'balloon construction'. It enabled builders to erect new houses much more quickly, and helped to end the misery of the early industrial towns.

Washington Roebling is the engineer of New York's Brooklyn suspension bridge. Paralysed and ill, he oversees its construction from his sick-room. His instructions are passed to the workmen by his wife who, in 1883, is given the honour of being the first person to cross the bridge (despite a superstition that, because she is a woman, it would therefore be cursed).

The Money Men

The need to raise large amounts of money to build the railways led to the growth of the stock exchanges, such as the Bourse in Paris and Wall Street in New York, where 'shares' in companies (called joint stock companies) were sold to the public. Ordinary people invested their money both at home and abroad through the stock exchanges. By 1914, Britons had put £4,000 million into overseas loans, and French investors had lent £1,850 million – much of it to Germany, their arch-rival. In this way the savings of millions of people financed economic growth all over the world.

The joint stock companies, however, often went bankrupt, ruining thousands of small investors. Some directors did not hesitate to use other people's money to make themselves wealthy. Others, such as the American financier Jay Gould, 'played the stock exchange'. He called his method 'profit through destruction', and his treatment of the Union Pacific Railway Company in 1873 shows how it worked. First, Gould published articles in his newspaper, the *New York World*, undermining confidence in the company. Eventually the price of its shares collapsed (this he called a 'bear raid'). Gould bought a majority holding of the firm's shares. Having gained control of the company, he made it buy, at a very high price, two railways he owned. Then his newspaper praised the company until the price of its shares rose, and finally he sold his shares, claiming to have done the public a great favour by returning so valuable a company to thousands of 'widows, orphans and lady stockholders'.

People with a little money to spare put it into a savings bank, which invests the money and pays them interest. The banks, however, are notoriously unstable and often go bankrupt. Here, during a 'run on the banks', angry creditors try to withdraw their money after hearing that the bank has invested in a business venture that is about to fail.

The Second Revolution

One modern historian has described the second half of the nineteenth century as a time when science 'broke the mould of established explanation' about how the world worked.

In 1859 the English naturalist Charles Darwin published *The Origin of Species by Natural Selection*. Darwin argued that living creatures had developed through a process of evolution, whereby those species most 'fitted' to their environment survived and prospered. It aroused a massive controversy, as it was used to attack the teaching of the Church that God created the world (at 9 o'clock on Monday morning, 23 October, 4004 BC, according to the vice-chancellor of Cambridge University).

Chemistry advanced considerably. In the eighteenth century, chemists had learned how to isolate oxygen and chlorine (1774), how to obtain alkali (1791), and how to produce gas from coal (1792). In 1859 the first synthetic dye (magenta) was produced from coal-tar. In 1860 an international chemical congress standardized names and symbols for the elements.

Physics also progressed. In 1873 the Belgian engineer Zenobe Gramme invented an effective electric motor/generator. In 1876, in America, Alexander Graham Bell patented the telephone and Thomas Edison invented the gramophone. Three years later, Edison developed a working light bulb. Radio waves were discovered in 1883 (by the German physicist, Heinrich Hertz). At that time scientists believed that these waves passed

through a substance they called 'ether', but all attempts to isolate it failed. This caused a debate which eventually led to Einstein's Theory of Relativity in 1905, and a completely new way of thinking about the universe.

Industrial Change

The inventions of the early industrial revolution had been made by ingenious mechanics (although some modern historians argue that science played an important part even in this period). After 1850, however, there was much greater emphasis on science, as engineers explored how to use the new scientific knowledge in industry. German industrialists employed research experts specifically to develop new methods of production. Historians have called this period of applied science the 'second Industrial Revolution' – a revolution based on gas, oil, electricity and chemical engineering.

An alkali was needed to make soap; coaltar dyes were used in cloth-making. Chloroform was used as an anaesthetic, iodine as an antiseptic, and chlorine as a bleach. Phosphorus was used to make matches. German scientists discovered how phosphates and superphosphates improved the soil's fertility.

Coal-gas (extracted by burning coal) had been used on a small scale for lighting and heating since the early nineteenth century. In the second half of the century, it was extensively used in the home for heating, lighting and cooking. Many towns began to make their streets safer, and reduced crime, by introducing gas lighting. In 1876 a German engineer, Nicholas Otto, built an efficient four-stroke gas engine and sold 30,000 of them in ten years. There was a boom in investment in gasworks between 1865 and 1885.

Another new fuel, petroleum, started to become available in the United States after the discovery of the Pennsylvania oilfields in 1859. It was used for lighting, and also for lubrication; and gasoline (refined petroleum) was used as a medicine. By 1917 nearly half a million oil wells had been sunk in America.

Meanwhile, electrical engineers were finding practical uses for electricity. New methods of communication were developed: the electric telegraph (1837; see page 29), telephones (1876; see page 36) and the wireless (1896). The first electric tram went into service in Berlin in 1881.

Electricity was increasingly used for lighting because it was cleaner and less dangerous than gas or oil. By 1882 Edison had installed more than 150 electrical generators in houses, hotels, mills and ships; in that year central generating stations were opened in London (Holborn) and New York (Pearl Street).

Above left: Thomas Edison in his laboratory.

  Above: Guglielmo Marconi, the inventor of the wireless.

  Far left: the transmitter from which the first BBC radio broadcast (a news bulletin) was made in 1922.

Trade and Transport

Trade was the basis of the wealth of the countries of industrialized Europe. Above all, they needed food to feed their growing populations. The British imported wheat from Argentina (in February and March), Australia (April), India (May, June and July), the American West (August and September), Russia (October) and Canada (during the winter). The invention of tin cans and refrigeration allowed ships to bring even perishable goods from all over the world. In addition, the European countries needed markets (somewhere to sell their products) and sources of raw materials (to supply their manufacturing industries).

Any country that did not want to trade with the industrial powers was forced to do so. The western nations had mechanized warfare as well as industry and this – particularly the gunboat and the machine gun – gave them a military advantage.

Britain was the country most prepared to bully less advanced nations. The English author of a book written in 1844 imagined a Turkish military official describing with awe British steamships and trains: 'The armies of the English ride upon the vapours of boiling cauldrons, and their horses are flaming coals. Whirr! Whirr! All by wheels! All by steam… The ships of the English swarm like flies; their printed calicoes cover the whole earth… All India is but an item in the ledger-books of the merchants.'

In 1838, when the Chinese government seized 20,291 chests of the illegal drug opium from British traders, the British government sent in the navy. The Chinese were forced to 'lease' Hong Kong to Britain, and to allow the British to trade in China (1842).

The Suez Canal in Egypt (opened in 1869) shortens the journey between India and western Europe by 4,000 miles (6,400 kilometres). In 1875 the British government buys a controlling interest in the canal. This action sparks off a 'scramble for colonies' in Africa.

Economic Forces

In the second half of the nineteenth century the Industrial Revolution spread out from the countries of western Europe (Britain, Belgium, France, Germany) and the United States. Germans set up business in Austria-Hungary, the Balkans and Turkey; they began planning a Berlin to Baghdad railway in 1888. French banks funded Russian industry, shipyards and banks. The United States invested millions of dollars in Cuba and Mexico.

These countries, however, found it much harder to have their own industrial revolution. Technology had advanced too far, and they could not afford the vast outlay on machines, factories, transport and communications that was necessary if they were to compete with the industrialized countries of the West. There were some successes: Sweden managed to use her vast resources of wood and iron to become an industrial power; Switzerland concentrated on highly priced, high-quality products; and Denmark, without coal or iron, achieved an agricultural revolution. Russia and Austria-Hungary, however, struggled to develop, and the rest of the world remained backward.

The non-industrialized areas of the world were at the mercy of European and American businessmen. They bought manufactured goods from the West and paid for them by supplying large amounts of raw materials at the lowest possible price. In this way they came to be dominated economically by the industrialized countries.

Imperialism

As the century progressed, competition between the industrialized nations became increasingly fierce. The United States and Germany began to move ahead of Britain. In 1895 a book by E.E. Williams, called *Made in Germany*, claimed that Britain was losing her position as 'workshop of the world'. German trade with Japan, the author said, had increased 500 per cent in the last seven years.

The answer, clearly, was not only to open up world markets but also to close them to competitors. The best way to do this was to conquer the countries concerned. At the same time there was a growing 'jingoism' in the industrialized nations – a feeling that they were superior to other nations. The English poet Rudyard Kipling urged his readers to take up the 'white man's burden' to civilize the rest of the world; hundreds of Christian missionaries who went abroad to 'convert the heathen' were part of this process.

The western powers, therefore, conquered less-developed countries to make them into colonies (part of their empires). After the 1830s the French government tried to 'revive the Roman Empire' in Africa; between 1862 and 1867 they annexed Indo-China. Between 1871 and 1900 Britain added 4,250,000 square miles (11 million square kilometres) and 66 million people to an Empire 'on which the sun never set'. In two years (1884-85)

Germany gained more than 350,000 square miles (905,000 square kilometres) of territory in Tanganyika in East Africa. In 1885 King Leopold of Belgium acquired almost a million square miles in the Congo; he then said that only Belgian companies could trade there.

The United States expanded aggressively – Texas was annexed in 1845, Oregon in 1846; a short war with Mexico added California, New Mexico, Nevada, Utah and Arizona in 1848; Alaska was purchased from Russia in 1867. Troops crushed those who resisted, such as the American Indians and the Mormons. To increase trade, the United States conquered the Spanish colonies of Puerto Rico, the Philippines and Hawaii (1898), and established 'protectorates' over Cuba and Panama.

When they had conquered an area, the colonial powers opened it up for trade. The British planned a railway from Cairo in Egypt to Cape Town in South Africa. The French wanted a railway across the Sahara. The Americans completed the lines across the Great Plains (see page 28), and in 1904 began the construction of the Panama Canal to open up trade routes with the Far East.

Imperialism was not all bad; it brought western legal systems, a civil service and efficient transport to the countries that were colonized. Imperialism, however, always gave the economic advantage to the conquerors. The industrial centres of the United States and western Europe took wool from Australia, gold from Alaska, diamonds from South Africa, rubber from Malaya, tea from India and corned beef from Argentina. The whole world had been mobilized to supply the industrial countries and to buy their manufactured goods.

Main picture: an official of the British Royal Niger Company with the people of the Katenu tribe of Nigeria in 1883. Two years later the British government declares the area a 'protectorate'.

Left: British forces destroy a native army at the Battle of Omdurman in the Sudan (1898).

Above left: the privileges of British rule in India.

Emigration

Europeans emigrated to populate the new lands opened up by imperialism. Between 1871 and 1911 approximately 28 million people left Europe for Australia and New Zealand, Brazil and Argentina, and Canada and the United States.

Many European industrialists set up small settlements of merchants in foreign ports. Swedish and German farmers sold their farms and bought land from the American railway companies – at $1.25 an acre. Many were attracted by *Beef Bonanza on the Plains, or How to Get Rich Quick*, a book written in 1881 by the American journalist James Brisbin. English farmers went to Australia or New Zealand seeking good pastureland; Welsh coalminers went to the Pennsylvania coalfields for higher wages. Italian peasants sold their houses to raise the money to go to work as unskilled labourers on the American railways. Gangs of Polish men, also, were contracted to work on the railways; they travelled in groups of ten, each gang taking an old woman to cook and wash for them.

Other emigrants were failures seeking a new start: bankrupt businessmen, impoverished nobles, and criminals on the run from the police. Some emigrants had their passage paid by their trade unions (see page 48), because their union activities had led to them being blacklisted at home. Irish peasants fled from starvation and poverty; Slovaks fled from political oppression in Hungary. From Russia came Jews, 'pathetic with the silent story of persecution'.

The emigrants found themselves in a strange and hostile environment. When English farmers in Wisconsin sang carols on Christmas Eve, other settlers panicked, thinking they were hearing the war cries of attacking Indians. Joining society at the bottom and despised as 'micks', 'wops', 'spics', 'polacks', and 'pommies', the newcomers clung together. Many became more fiercely nationalist than they had ever been at home; the American Irish saved their money and sent it back to Ireland to support the fight against the English.

Most emigrants were energetic, adaptable and intelligent (although not necessarily educated). By definition, they were people with 'get-up-and-go'. They worked hard, and their children benefited from their efforts. Often they paid for members of the family to come and join them, or sent money home to support an aged relative. The accompanying letters would be passed proudly round the whole village, and others would be encouraged to try their luck in the New World.

Above: off to a new life. Emigrants on their way to America, dancing happily on the deck of SS *Patricia* in 1902. The United States is the 'land of opportunity'; between 1871 and 1911 it attracts 20.5 million immigrants.

The emigrants, however, face a dangerous passage in the steerage (the cheapest accommodation) of an old ship. They must watch for sharpers (confidence tricksters). It is rumoured that some captains throw their passengers overboard unless they pay their fare again. Whole families sometimes die of hunger or disease and are buried at sea in shrouds made from an old sail (left).

The other emigrants gather round to watch. They include the kind of people listed as passengers on a ship leaving Bremen in Germany in 1890: a young German farmer going to join his brother in New Jersey; a German chair-maker who has had his ticket pre-paid by his brother in San Francisco; a Hungarian girl of 20, going to join her father in Wisconsin; and a Hungarian farmer going to join his brother in the Cleveland copperworks. They are united by one hope – that they will have a better life when they reach America.

Wealth

The Industrial Revolution created great wealth – for some people. Alfred Krupp became the wealthiest man in Germany. The American businessman J.P. Morgan left $80 million when he died. Such men easily gained entry to the upper classes. The daughter of the American industrialist Henry Singer (of Singer sewing machines) married the Prince de Polignac.

Beneath these super-rich people were the bourgeoisie. Some sociologists of the time divided them into 'upper middle class' (industrialists, bankers, lawyers and doctors) and 'lower middle class' (shopkeepers, craftsmen, teachers, civil servants and clerks).

Most middle-class families aspired to live in a detached house with a garden. In Boston, in the United States, one father advised his son: 'When you marry, pick out a suburb to build a house in, join the Country Club, and make your life center about your club, your home and your children.' The family of the economist J.M. Keynes was typically upper middle class. His father, the registrar of Cambridge University, earned £1,000 a year (of which he saved £400), employed three servants and a governess, took two holidays

a year (including a month in Switzerland), collected butterflies and played golf.

Middle-class families were usually religious (they often belonged to religious minorities such as the French Calvinists, British Quakers, or Austrian Jews) and most days began with the whole household, including the servants, praying together. Moral correctness was vital; an unmarried girl might kill herself if she became pregnant.

While the man of the house went to work in his office, his wife ran the household, bullied the tradesmen and organized the servants who looked after the children and did the housework. Occasionally, she might venture out in a horse-drawn cab to one of the new department stores. The law classed her as one of her husband's possessions and she would probably look on the idea of women's suffrage (the vote) with horror.

In some respects this middle-class lifestyle still influences the popular stereotype of what constitutes a 'happy family'.

This late-nineteenth-century German doll's house shows a typical wealthy middle-class household. The family live 'upstairs' in luxury. Servants are an essential mark of the family's wealth, but they work mainly 'below stairs' in the kitchen. On the top floor are the children's nursery and the servants' sleeping quarters.

Philanthropy

The role-model of the early Industrial Revolution was the self-made man. Many people believed that poverty was the result of drunkenness, idleness or low morals. Most industrialists believed in *laissez faire* ('let things be'), and opposed government intervention in the economy.

The process which reversed this attitude began in Britain with William Wilberforce's crusade against the slave trade (1787-1808). Then, in 1830, people who had supported Wilberforce read a letter in the *Leeds Mercury* from Richard Oastler, a land agent, who described 'a state of slavery [in the mills and mines of England] more horrid than that hellish system of Colonial Slavery'. This was the beginning of the nineteenth-century philanthropy (caring for others) among the middle classes.

By the end of the century many middle-class organizations were trying to improve the living and working standards of the poor. In England, Lord Shaftesbury spent all his life trying to improve working conditions, lunatic asylums and education. William Booth founded the Salvation Army in 1865. Thomas Barnardo opened the first of his children's homes in 1867. Even the Prime Minister, William Gladstone, to the horror of his friends, went out at night to find prostitutes, took them back to No. 10 Downing Street and tried to persuade them to change their ways.

In Russia the manager of the Krenholm cotton factory in Narva started the movement to reduce the hours of child labour (1867). In

Germany and Switzerland, large firms such as Krupp (armaments), Bayer (chemicals) and Suchard (chocolate) built 'model villages' with good housing and amenities for their workers. After 1896, at Elberfeld in Germany, the textile firm of Peters & Co. operated a welfare scheme which included a sickness fund, a savings bank, a pension fund, help with house purchase, a welfare institute for lectures and social events, public baths and showers, a steam laundry and a library.

In the United States, towards the end of the century, child labour committees, church organizations and women's clubs campaigned to improve conditions through changes in the law. Often women took the lead in these campaigns, as the movement grew which believed that women should become involved in philanthropic and political matters.

Meal time in a London orphanage in 1901. Conditions had improved greatly since the early nineteenth century, when the principle of English state poor relief had been that it must be so awful that it would be claimed only by those who were desperately in need.

Above left: during the nineteenth century many towns opened 'Free Libraries'. Here, workers in Manchester, England, read the latest news from America.

Unions, Parties and Laws

During the second half of the nineteenth century, the working classes began to organize themselves into groups to try to improve their situation.

There had been little working-class activism before 1850. In Britain the Chartists had organized a Charter (petition) demanding the vote, but it proved a fiasco. People had signed it with ridiculous false names such as 'Flatnose', 'No Cheese' and even 'Queen Victoria'; the name of the Duke of Wellington – in charge of the government's troops – appeared 17 times. In 1848 the Chartists marched to London. When they were asked not to cross the River Thames, however, they obediently agreed, sending the huge petition to Parliament in horse-drawn cabs.

Trade Unions

After 1850, however, the working classes became more assertive. They formed trade unions to fight for better wages and conditions for the workers. In Britain the first Trades Union Congress was held in 1868; by 1912 – a year in which 40 million working days were lost in strikes – there were 3.4 million trade unionists in Britain. In the same year the German Trades Union Congress (formed in 1892) had 2.5 million members. In the United States, an organization called The Industrial Workers of the World grew up after 1905. It wanted 'one big union' and

undertook a number of violent strikes. Meanwhile, membership of the American Federation of Labor grew fivefold between 1898 and 1904, although still only 10 per cent of the workforce belonged to trade unions by 1914.

Trade Unions did well during times of prosperity, because employers were prepared to meet the workers' demands. In times of depression, however, employers refused to give way and the workers tended to turn away from the unions. Instead, they started to become involved in politics.

Socialism

In 1848 Karl Marx (a German professor married to an aristocrat) and Friedrich Engels (the son of a factory owner) wrote *The Communist Manifesto*. In it they claimed that the workers of the world had become 'wage slaves' of the bourgeoisie, who not only owned the businesses but dominated the government. They urged the working classes to unite to overthrow the bourgeoisie – either by revolution, or (in countries where working men had the vote) by winning an election.

There were many different working-class political parties in Europe. Most were socialist (they believed that the state should own the means of production). The most extreme form of socialism was communism, and Marxism was the most important of the communist ideologies (theories).

In 1889 the Second International Working Men's Association met in Paris, with members from all over Europe and the United States – and even one from Japan. In 1900 the Labour Party was formed in Britain and five years later a socialist party was formed in France. In the Swedish elections of 1907, Social Democrats gained 64 seats out of 230. In 1912 Eugene Debs, a socialist railway-union leader, ran for president in the United States' election and received nearly a million votes.

By 1912 the German Social Democratic Party (founded in 1875) had four million supporters and was the largest party in the German *Reichstag* (parliament).

Laws

Organized into strong unions and large political parties, working-class people were able to campaign for changes in the law. In an attempt to prevent them from becoming socialist, governments adopted legislation which would benefit the workers. The German government introduced health insurance (1883) and old age pensions (1889), specifically to 'check the spread of socialism' and prevent a revolution. In Britain the Third Reform Act (1884) gave the vote to all men over the age of 21, and by 1914 the government had introduced unemployment benefits, national health insurance and old age pensions. The French government regulated hours of work (1892), gave free medical treatment (1893) and introduced child allowances (1913). In the years after 1903, American states brought in laws restricting the number of hours children and women could work, setting minimum wages for women, and establishing workers' compensation.

Workers slowly began to benefit from the Industrial Revolution. Real wages (money wages, taking account of the changes in prices) increased by over 50 per cent in Britain and Germany between 1850 and 1914. Increased sales of items such as sugar and meat also indicated gradually increasing wealth.

Nevertheless, there was still great financial inequality between the classes. According to a 1906 survey, 0.5 per cent of the population of Great Britain (a quarter of a million people) owned one-third of the nation's wealth.

Below: striking iron workers march for higher wages.
Far left: the union leader Mary MacArthur speaking to box-makers in Trafalgar Square, London, in 1908.

Education

Gradually, changes were made which improved people's lives. Change happened first where not only the workers but also the government and industrialists could hope to benefit. Education was one such area.

In Britain, in 1841, a Parliamentary Commission had met boys who had never heard of London and thought the Queen's name was Prince Albert. Few had heard of Jesus Christ. 'Does 'e work down the pit?' asked one miner. They could not read, write or do the simplest sums.

Between 1870 and 1914 some form of education was made compulsory in most of Europe and the United States. The number of primary school teachers trebled in Sweden; in Finland the number of primary school children increased thirteenfold.

The German schools, which put great emphasis on practical, technical and scientific subjects, were acknowledged to be 'far ahead of any other country'. England lagged behind; secondary education was mostly private and consisted mainly of Latin, Greek and competitive sports.

Few people found that education was 'a ladder from the gutter to the university along which any child may climb'. Education often reinforced class divisions. A boy from a wealthy family would go to university. Having graduated, he would join the Old Boys' Association (the *Korps* in Germany or the fraternity in the United States) and would mix with people from the same background as his own. In 1889 the American fraternity *Delta Kappa Epsilon* included bankers and businessmen, as well as six senators, 40 congressmen and Theodore Roosevelt (who in 1901 became President of the United States).

Meanwhile, governments and industrialists saw education as a way of preparing working-

class children for the army and the factory. In France, primary school teachers were instructed 'not to let pupils get habits, tastes and ideas which will separate them from the manner of life and work for which they are intended'. In 1877 the American Commissioner of Education hoped that 'schools could train the children to resist the evils of strikes and violence'. In Germany, a royal command of 1889 instructed teachers 'to establish in the minds of those who are still young, that socialism is against Christianity…and that the working classes can only trust the Kaiser [emperor] for justice and the safety of their wages'.

Most schoolwork is dull and consists of memorizing lists of facts. Here, German pupils have finished an algebra lesson and are about to start reading.

The teacher is a stern disciplinarian; punishments include the cane, shackling pupils to the desk, hanging logs round their necks, putting them in a basket hanging from the roof, and parading them round the school wearing a tin or paper hat.

Der Frühling Der Herbst

Der Sommer

$$a = 3$$
$$2(a+5) = b$$
$$b = 16$$

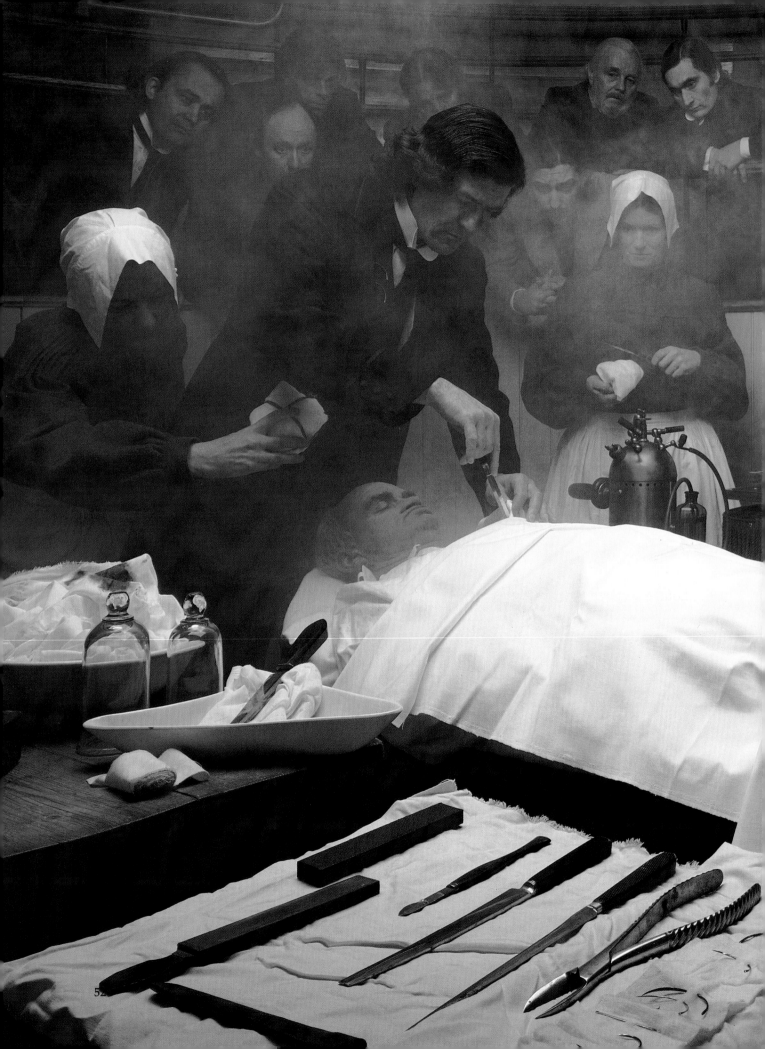

Medicine and Health

Until about 1860, in the words of one nurse, hospitals did 'more harm than good'. Many patients died of blood poisoning. Before the introduction of anaesthetics, surgeons rushed through operations to limit the pain. The British surgeon Robert Liston could amputate a leg in two and a half minutes. He once cut off not only the patient's leg, but the fingers of the assistant holding him down; both died later of blood poisoning. Liston also slashed the coat of a spectator, who dropped dead of fright. According to the medical writer Richard Gordon, it was 'the only operation in history with a 300 per cent mortality'!

Meanwhile, the cholera epidemics of 1830 and 1848 – which spread into the suburbs where the wealthy lived – led to an outcry for something to be done about public health. Governments were alarmed because a large proportion of army volunteers were unfit for military service. Industrialists hoped production would improve if fewer working days were lost through sickness.

The turning point came in 1864 when Louis Pasteur, a French chemist, proved that germs cause disease. Now they knew what was causing the problem, governments could introduce laws to improve public health and town planning. Germany led the way. Many German towns adopted 'municipal socialism' (town socialism), financing the building of sewers, gasworks and waterworks. By the end of the century, epidemics of diseases such as cholera and typhoid had become a thing of the past in the West.

Anaesthetics – laughing gas (1800), ether (1842) and chloroform (1847) – and anti-septics improved the patient's chances of surviving surgery. Other inventions – for instance, aspirin, X-rays and the electro-cardiograph (which records heartbeats) – improved medical care. In the years after 1854, Florence Nightingale reformed the nursing profession in Britain, and laid down standards for hygiene in hospitals.

Doctors began trying to cure infectious diseases. During the 1870s a German medical officer, Robert Koch, discovered how to use coal-tar dyes to colour germs, thereby showing which germ caused which disease. In the 1880s, Pasteur's team of French scientists discovered how to inoculate against disease (injecting a weakened form of the germ to allow the body to build up its defences). Teams of scientists tried to find chemical substances that would attack and kill germs; the German doctor Paul Ehrlich discovered that the compound Salvarsan 606 cured syphilis (a sexually transmitted disease).

Sewers and clean tap water; inoculation against diseases such as tuberculosis and diphtheria; painkillers; going into hospital and being cured – these things were virtually unknown before the Industrial Revolution. During the nineteenth century the discoveries were made which allowed them to become commonplace today. Their contribution to the quality of our lives is incalculable.

Left: an operation at St Thomas's Hospital, London, in 1862. Anaesthetics make the operation painless. To kill the germs, surgeons disinfect their surgical instruments, and drench themselves, their patients and the operating theatre in a fine spray of carbolic acid.

Below: building a sewer in east London in 1859. Sewers and clean water save many more lives than all the other improvements in medical care put together.

Home Helps

'Thirty morning gowns; now I call that real happiness,' comments the upper-class heroine of a novel written by an English woman in 1830. 'Not such real, lasting happiness as eighteen bracelets, heaps of gloves and handkerchiefs…and going to be married,' replies her friend. The lives of most wealthy women consisted mainly of needlework, painting, playing the piano, and dressing for the evening meal. Some were happy; others felt frustrated and unfulfilled: 'Oh weary days – oh evenings that never seem to end – and for 20, 30 years more to do this,' wrote Florence Nightingale, before an income of £500 a year from her father enabled her to leave home.

Women and girls from poor families often worked in the factories or were servants in upper-class and middle-class households. However, in middle-class families (and in more and more working-class families that aspired to be middle class) the husbands went out to work while their wives stayed at home. These women were tied to the house and totally dependent on their husbands; to 'make a man's home delightful' was their main duty. Mrs Beeton wrote *Household Management* (1861) for such women, so that their husbands would find their homes more attractive than the pub!

After 1870, however, the position of women slowly began to change. Even though birth control was frowned upon (when the English union leader Annie Besant supported it, the courts took away her children), families began to have fewer children. Wives, no longer continuously pregnant, were freed to do other things. Education laws meant that all girls received some schooling. Some went to secondary school and even to university – although most men disapproved of 'blue stockings' (educated women).

Middle-class women started to go out to work. Compulsory education opened up teaching as a possible career. Women became typists and telephonists. A few became doctors, authors and journalists. Women joined the new socialist parties, formed unions, ran Christian missions in working-class areas, and campaigned against 'the demon drink'. In the United States, the General Federation of Women's Clubs fought for better living and working conditions.

Attitudes changed. By the end of the nineteenth century strong-willed American women known as 'titanesses' went to nightclubs and danced the tango. In Austria, society women wore revealing V-necked dresses and smoked cigars. In England they wore 'bonnets, loud stockings, capes, crinolines and ringlets straying over the shoulder, better known by the name of "follow me, lads"', to attract the men. In Russia, liberated upper-class women believed in free love (sex without marriage). By 1914, women had the vote in Australia, Norway, New Zealand and some American states; in England and the rest of the United States, 'suffragettes' were campaigning for it.

Left: new technology in the home. The flat-iron gives way to the electric iron (1909), needle and thread to the sewing machine (1851) and dustpan and brush to the vacuum cleaner (1903). Washing machines (1880s) replace the washboard; refrigerators (1860) replace the meat safe; gas cookers (1880) replace the kitchen range.

Right: clothing becomes looser (the brassiere replaces whalebone corsets) and gives women more freedom of movement.

Mass Appeal

To the German philosopher Nietzsche it seemed that in the late nineteenth century cultural interests (such as art, music and literature) were under attack from two quarters – 'the mob and the eccentrics'.

Fashionable young people wanted to be *avant-garde* (ahead of the rest). Everything was 'new' – the new woman, *art nouveau*, *Neue Zeit* (*New Age*, the title of a Marxist newspaper). Painters such as Monet and Van Gogh (members of a group of artists known as the Impressionists) broke away from the idealized realism of earlier artists. For wealthy women, there were even new diseases – tennis elbow and bicycle face.

Improved communications had made the world a smaller place. Middle-class families wanted to show off their knowledge of new playwrights such as Ibsen, Shaw and Chekhov. There were crazes for some aspects of foreign culture – Negro blues, Spanish flamenco and the Argentinian tango.

The monotonous routine of compulsory education did not often teach children to appreciate cultural things, but it taught them that they ought to appreciate those things if they wanted to better themselves; this was the great age of social snobbery. In Germany the number of theatres trebled between 1870 and 1896. Huge audiences watched opera stars such as the Great Caruso, an Italian, and

Dame Nellie Melba (an Australian singer so popular that she had an ice-cream dessert named after her). The German composer Wagner caught the feeling of German nationalism. Imperialistic British audiences at the London Promenade Concerts (started in 1895) joined in to sing Elgar's *Land of Hope and Glory* and *Rule Britannia*.

As wages gradually increased, working-class people had more money to spend on entertainment. In the towns, a working-class culture developed, which included cycling, baseball and soccer clubs, music halls and beer halls, cafés, pubs and brass bands. Films, a fairground novelty in 1895, attracted audiences of 50 million a week in the United States by 1914.

Above: an advertisement encouraging the upper and middle classes to take their holidays abroad; less wealthy people would take a train to the seaside.

Below: early films have to be shot in daylight.

Big Business

During the 1860s Herbert Spencer, the first sociologist, applied Darwin's ideas about 'the survival of the fittest' to business.

Spencer's philosophy was accepted most enthusiastically in the United States. Competition was cut-throat. The American businessman John D. Rockefeller forced smaller companies to merge with his Standard Oil Company until, by 1879, he controlled 90 per cent of the oil-refining industry. He built pipelines to avoid using the railways. He used his own tankers, made his own barrels, manufactured the oil lamps. Then he bought out the retailers and sold the oil himself.

American management methods led the world. The principles of 'scientific management' were worked out by H.W. Taylor, the originator of time and motion studies, in 1911. To motivate their workforce, many American firms also introduced personnel departments, canteens, social clubs and profit sharing.

American businessmen turned the Industrial Revolution into big business. They formed huge corporations and powerful cartels (whereby firms co-operate to fix prices and destroy opposition). In 1912 three men – J.P. Morgan (see page 44), George Baker of the First National Bank, and James Stillman of the National City Bank – controlled 112 companies worth over $22,000 million.

'The young American appears to be continually possessed by a determination to become something "big"', wrote an English visitor to New York in 1882. To work your way from poverty to riches – like Rockefeller, Andrew Carnegie (steel), George Pullman (railways) or Jay Gould (finance) – was the 'American dream'.

American businessmen revolutionize production methods. In 1913, Henry Ford starts to mass-produce his Model T Ford car on a moving assembly line. It comes only in black. In 1914 Ford produces 248,000 cars costing as little as $490 each, and makes a profit of over $30 million. The motor car provides millions of people with a hitherto unknown freedom of travel.

Into the Future

To many people, the twentieth century has seemed a golden age of advance: a sequence of marvels including aeroplanes (1903), plastics (1908), television (1925), nylon (1937), the computer (1948), nuclear power (1956), heart transplants (1967), a moon landing (1969), and 'test-tube' babies (1978).

Yet the Industrial Revolution has created problems that we are unable to solve. In *Limits to Growth* (1972), the Massachusetts Institute of Technology has forecast the destruction of the human life-system during the twenty-first century as a result of pollution, the population explosion and over-use of the world's natural resources. The sexual revolution (see page 55) seems to threaten the role of the family as the basis of society. Nuclear weapons have given state leaders the power to destroy every living thing on earth dozens of times over.

In the industrialized countries there are minority groups – often racial minorities – which feel excluded from the benefits of industrialization. They form a bitter 'out-group' with their own sub-culture (which often includes drugs and violence). Dis-enchanted by progress, others want to 'drop out of the rat race'.

Although certain Far Eastern countries

such as Japan, Taiwan and Hong Kong have managed to compete with the industrialized nations of the West, it is very difficult for a non-industrialized country to have an industrial revolution. Not only is the 'technological leap' greater than ever, but the industrialized countries are organized into economic communities which effectively exclude others. Many Third World countries also believe that western concerns about pollution and the over-use of resources are a trick to stop them industrializing as well.

While the western world feasts, others starve. The United States – which contains only 6 per cent of the world's population – uses 33 per cent of its oil, 44 per cent of its coal and 63 per cent of its gas. One writer comments: 'It is obvious that the world cannot afford the USA. Nor can it afford Western Europe or Japan – the rich who are using all the marvellous achievements of science and technology to indulge in a crude materialistic way of life which ravages the earth. The problem passengers on Spaceship Earth are the first-class passengers and no one else.'

Putting the inventions of the Industrial Revolution to destructive ends: the armies of the First World War use aeroplanes first for reconnaissance (below), and later as fighters and bombers. Nitrate of ammonia (a fertilizer) is used for explosive shells, chlorine (a disinfectant used in hospitals) for poisonous gas, and coal-tar dyes to colour soldiers' uniforms.

How Do We Know?

On Wednesday 15 September, 1830, Fanny Kemble rode on the railway. She was nineteen years old, and the experience thrilled her: 'What with the sight and sound of these cheering crowds and the tremendous speed [10 miles/16 kilometres per hour] my spirits rose to champagne height.' Her mother, however, was 'frightened to death'.

How do we know? Because Miss Kemble wrote it all down in a letter. Reading it today, historians can learn about the opening day of the first passenger railway and the attitudes of those who were present.

A tiny fraction of many such sources has been used in this book: for example, a German textile worker's description of life in a Berlin house (see pages 26-27); and Florence Nightingale's outburst of frustration in her diary (page 55). As more people learned to read and write, even working-class people could write down their feelings (see page 25).

Novels by writers such as Charles Dickens (1812-70) and Émile Zola (1840-1902) also offer vivid details of the environment and attitudes of the time. However, historians must remember that these accounts are subjective (they reflect the authors' opinions).

Some contemporary sources are, nevertheless, carefully researched, objective accounts (they attempt to be fair). Edward Baines' *History of the Cotton Manufacture* (1835), for example, is still a valuable source of information. In it he recorded an interview with Edmund Cartwright (see page 14), and his statements about the textile revolution (see page 13) are considered opinions, not personal prejudices. Dr Villermé (see page 24) and Dr Guépin (see page 26), who wrote about the lives of French factory workers, visited and interviewed individuals, as well as using government statistics.

The number of newspapers, such as the *Leeds Mercury* (see page 46), increased throughout the nineteenth century. Historians can also investigate the account books and correspondence books of individual firms. A single sentence on page 21 of this book, for instance, was based on a mass of such information about the Whessoe Foundry in Darlington, England.

Historians can read a decree made by the German Kaiser in 1889 or a circular of 1893 written by a French education minister (see page 51). Every ten years after 1851 the British government took a census recording the name, age, marital status, position in the household, occupation and place of birth of every person in Great Britain. So many government reports exist that an historian could not read them in a lifetime. British Parliamentary Commissions recorded the ignorance of workers in 1841 (see page 50) and the fear felt by small children in the mines (see page 17). The description of emigrants leaving Bremen in 1890 (see page 43) is taken from a US Special Consular Report.

In 1841 an Englishman, Fox Talbot, patented the calotype, the forerunner of the photograph; you can see examples of early photographs on pages 28-29 and 58-59. After 1895 it was possible to take 'moving pictures' (see page 57). Meanwhile, the legacy of the Industrial Revolution can be seen everywhere – for instance, the Eiffel Tower in Paris and the Brooklyn Bridge in New York (see page 32), as well as railways, factories and steel mills. Details of life can be seen in industrial museums, although historians must remember that some do not merely preserve the remains of the past but try to reconstruct 'life as it used to be'. If this is the case, the reconstruction is an interpretation by a modern historian and may not be correct.

Using the Sources

For an historian investigating the years before 1800, the problem is to piece together a picture of what life was like from scraps of evidence. After 1800, problems arise because there are too many sources. Historians have to generalize from a mass of information. This can be difficult where the sources disagree as violently as Dr Villermé and Andrew Ure about factory children (see page 24). The historian has to consult as many sources as possible and try to come to a fair decision.

Not all sources are equally reliable. Sometimes writers let their prejudices affect their comments – for instance, the German writer who thought the Poles were poor because they were lazy (see page 9). The English writer Alexander Kinglake probably did not correctly express the views of a Turkish military official (see page 39). We cannot know whether the two heroines on page 55 were typical of all English girls of the time, or whether these were the views only of the author.

Even government sources are not always reliable. The British Commission of 1832 on factory conditions was led by Michael Sadler, a keen reformer. It *set out* to prove that conditions were terrible. One of the witnesses – quoted in many history books – was Samuel Coulson, a factory worker. He claimed that, for six weeks when the mill was busy, his children had worked 19 hours a day and had only 3 hours' sleep. Do you believe him?

Sometimes people altered the evidence for the best motives. A book published for the British Ladies Society in about 1835 included a picture of a cotton mill (above right, top). The artist who drew the pictures for *Michael Armstrong, Factory Boy* (1840) – a moralistic novel about the hardships of factory workers' lives – based one of his illustrations (middle) on this picture. Twenty years later another artist, who was illustrating *White Slaves of England*, further changed the picture to show the need for factory reform (bottom). The historian has to decide which picture best illustrates conditions in the factories. How would you decide?

Your Task

Historians used to think that if they found out all the facts, they could discover 'the truth' about the past. Nowadays, we believe that each new generation selects the facts it wants and uses them to develop new theories.

You can start now. Choose any page of this book, and ask in your local library for books of primary sources (sources from the time) about that topic. Read the sources and use them to criticize the statements in this book. Who says *I* have made the right interpretation?

Index

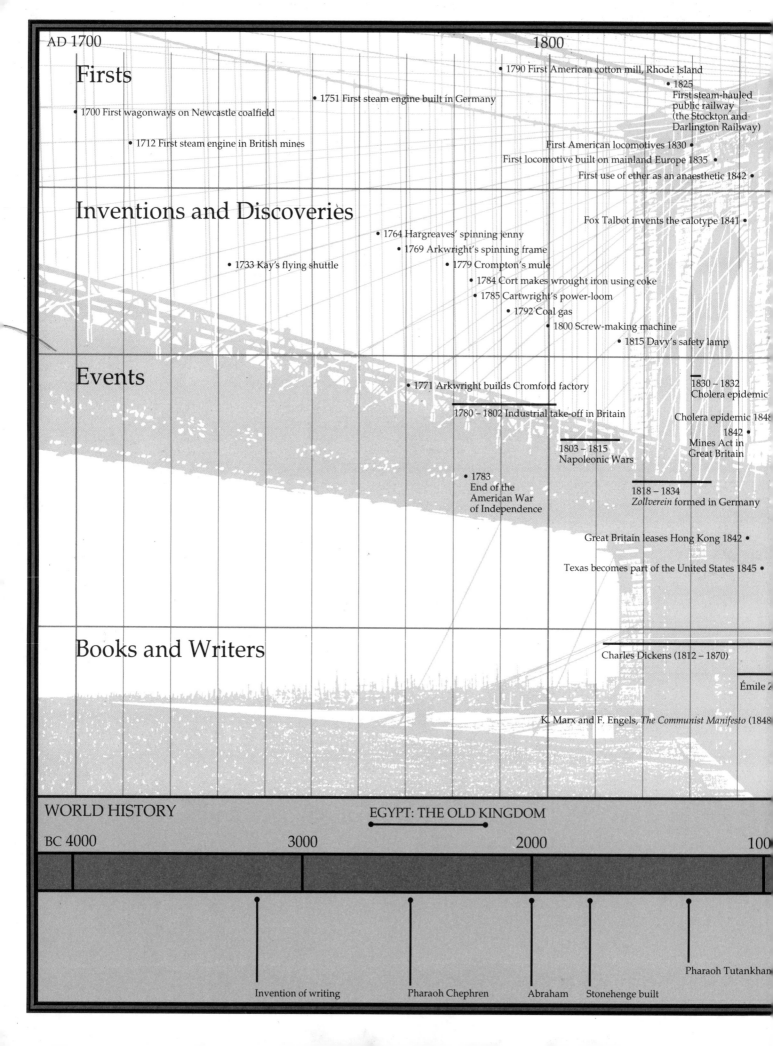

AD 1700   1800

Firsts

• 1790 First American cotton mill, Rhode Island
                                                            • 1825
                                        • 1751 First steam engine built in Germany   First steam-hauled
                                                            public railway
• 1700 First wagonways on Newcastle coalfield   (the Stockton and
                                                            Darlington Railway)

    • 1712 First steam engine in British mines   First American locomotives 1830 •
                                          First locomotive built on mainland Europe 1835 •
                                              First use of ether as an anaesthetic 1842 •

Inventions and Discoveries

                                                    Fox Talbot invents the calotype 1841 •

                                • 1764 Hargreaves' spinning jenny
                                  • 1769 Arkwright's spinning frame
        • 1733 Kay's flying shuttle   • 1779 Crompton's mule
                                      • 1784 Cort makes wrought iron using coke
                                        • 1785 Cartwright's power-loom
                                          • 1792 Coal gas
                                            • 1800 Screw-making machine
                                              • 1815 Davy's safety lamp

Events

                                                            1830 – 1832
                          • 1771 Arkwright builds Cromford factory   Cholera epidemic

                          ————————————————   Cholera epidemic 1848
                          1780 – 1802 Industrial take-off in Britain
                                                            1842 •
                                                            Mines Act in
                                          1803 – 1815   Great Britain
                                          Napoleonic Wars
                    • 1783
                    End of the
                    American War   1818 – 1834
                    of Independence   Zollverein formed in Germany

                                    Great Britain leases Hong Kong 1842 •

                                Texas becomes part of the United States 1845 •

Books and Writers

                                                    ————————————
                                          Charles Dickens (1812 – 1870)

                                                            Émile Z

                                K. Marx and F. Engels, *The Communist Manifesto* (1848

WORLD HISTORY   EGYPT: THE OLD KINGDOM

BC 4000   3000   2000   100

              Invention of writing   Pharaoh Chephren   Abraham   Stonehenge built

                                                            Pharaoh Tutankhan